THE LAST OF ENGLAND

*Peter Porter*

# THE LAST OF ENGLAND

LONDON
OXFORD UNIVERSITY PRESS
*New York   Melbourne*
1970

*Oxford University Press, Ely House, London W.1*

GLASGOW NEW YORK TORONTO MELBOURNE WELLINGTON
CAPE TOWN SALISBURY IBADAN NAIROBI DAR ES SALAAM LUSAKA ADDIS ABABA
BOMBAY CALCUTTA MADRAS KARACHI LAHORE DACCA
KUALA LUMPUR SINGAPORE HONG KONG TOKYO

SBN 19 211295 3

PRINTED IN GREAT BRITAIN BY
THE BOWERING PRESS PLYMOUTH

To
the memory of
my Mother
and
the decade of
the Nineteen Thirties

# ACKNOWLEDGEMENTS

ACKNOWLEDGEMENTS are due to the editors of the following periodicals in which some of these poems first appeared: *Ambit, Clare, Delos, Katawakes, The Listener, London Magazine, Micromegas, New Statesman, Phoenix, Poetry Book Society Christmas Supplement, 1967, Poetry Review,* and *Quarry*; and to The B.B.C. in whose programmes some others were read.

# CONTENTS

# THE LAST OF ENGLAND

It's quiet here among the haunted tenses:
Dread Swiss germs pass the rabbit's throat,
Chemical rain in its brave green hat
Drinks at a South Coast Bar, the hedgehog
Preens on nylon, we dance in Tyrolean
Drag whose mothers were McGregors,
Exiled seas fill every cubit of the bay.

Sailing away from ourselves, we feel
The gentle tug of water at the quay—
Language of the liberal dead speaks
From the soil of Highgate, tears
Show a great water table is intact.
You cannot leave England, it turns
A planet majestically in the mind.

# THE CIVIL WAR

Calm lie the plains of golden races,
Dark the forest where Europe died:
The Counter Reformation takes a bride,
The Container Revolution is a war—
No man's hand may be held against his neighbour,
Same against same is what the same is for,
The hire of death is worthy of the labour.

# ELEGY

Matriculated at last from strangeness,
inhabiting footfall and timetable,
not skirting broken glass or the well-kept
hedge that harbours a face in its midst,
       he launches himself on the city
       through a surf of man-made fibres,
       home again, the out-of-phase prodigal,
       ready to consume aggression and silence.

But things have changed in his absence—
the Commune is packed with priests and breakfasts,
talks on God are issued as supplements
and four times out of five the man-in-the-street
       recognizes Savonarola's picture:
       alas, the doctors are still over-
       prescribing, a furious novelist
       says she fucks for her health's sake.

What is he to make of Pan's Festival
where the corona and bays are awarded
unanimously to the Laureates of Low Spirits
and a group of formation dancers
       called Maud is interpreting scansion,
       where the vatic confessional
       is booked for the evening and Positive
       Evil is seriously on the syllabus?

How he hails them, the Comforters and Old-Time
Resistors he remembers from many a march:
they turn away and hand him a journal
with obscenities reversed out on pink paper;
       a page of the telephone directory
       serves as a libretto; someone says
       An American Machine is coming
       with Hot Gothic printed on its brow.

And even the home discomforts are not
quite what he remembers. The pigeons
still eat his herb garden and Consommé
the cat has bald patches—but, alas, the sweep
         of headlights on his bedroom wall
         is a flash of pain now, the porter's
         habit of reading his letters and hiding
         the envelopes no longer seems out of Gogol.

There is nowhere to go: the cars are nose to tail
along the Ring Road and every third remembered
café or pub is an estate agent's. La Bella
Bona Roba he had called her until he heard
         her order scampi and chips.
         Is it indeed time to attempt
         the serious novels he was keeping
         for his real old age?

Outside his window the trees perform their ritual
leaf-shedding in the month of the setting-up
of a Ministry of Technology. A world of lasars
has millions who must be blanket-bathed,
         and a species of rat-like marsupial
         is officially declared extinct—
         the Ars Nova sound is a special
         test of high-fidelity equipment.

A balm for these distracted times, he says—
a legend in my own garden, I shall stay
on the bench in what passes for evening sun
till I am stylite with air and crisis.
         Tell the neighbours the news—
         I come from a factory of the mad
         but I am at home to my mother
         the city. She will come to me.

4

# A MEREDITHIAN TREATMENT

We knew at the time that he was dangerous,
I for one had an instinctive loathing—
The dirt, the bells, the glasses tied with string—
Yet we thought of this as something wrong with us.
The past is dead, the future dead, the now
Is here, an apotheosis of girls begins.
He who takes nothing stronger than aspirins
Leads us in worship of the Dulcet Cow,
A sociologist issues us with parts!
I am King Pentheus, I shall sort out Thebes;
It's not the queers and chewers of poppy seeds
I hate, it's that gammony gang of tarts
That's bringing normal sex into disrepute;
They've read the legend wrong, my mother's torn
Me apart already, now I am reborn
In huge respectability, with a gun in my suit.

# CHRISTENINGS

The Good Fairies have trooped off one by one,
Their strawberry smiles fading and their
Consumer Durables piled up on the floor.
Here come the Baddies with their stingy gifts,
Small genitals they bring, bow legs, catarrh,
A talent for crosswords and losing girls,
For overhearing insults, getting gossip wrong,
Their Diners Cards make fatherly waiters rude,
What mother says they weep away in bed,
They throw your hat from the ferry when you're drunk:
To us, their godchildren, they give this saw,
A starlight epitaph—*Here they belong*
*Who died so young although they lived so long.*

# SHORT STORY

Maureen makes a rope and ribbon model
of Nicholas, plaiting him a big member,
          then puts it on to cook.

Her stove is patented 'The White Goddess'.

Nick is, as the novelists say,
          an ordinary, young, good-looking,
empty, ambitious, self-fascinated shit.

          I think we'll give Maureen
a weekly Group Analysis session.

Dr. Brandeis is away at a conference,
          what is she going to do?

Puts 67 barbiturates in a tumbler
          just to look at them.

Nick's saying to Mr. Ballantine,
          'terrific, I'm screwing this bird
and her bloody dog comes up and licks my balls.'

          Maureen enters a dream,
a pride of lions walks from the upturned glass—
          over their prophetic thighs
          puffs the angel of death.

'If she had to go for pills why couldn't
          she make it *the* Pill.'

The lions are in front of plexiglass
sunning in the architect's patio,
noiselessly they cross the nursing home
          and sip her quiet milk.

7

The Samaritans send her Norman O. Brown.

She could become an assistant
        with Abacus:
no, I'll set her up cataloguing
maiolica in a private collection.

    I'm going to give Nick
a mild dose, but I can't stop him
        becoming Brand Manager.

    I'm wearing God's shirt.

We'll leave Maureen under the departure board
at Waterloo looking up a train to Godalming.

The trouble is you can't write about dreams.

What was caught in Surrey in the headlights?

    This all came about because I had
    a strong letter asking me
    why not write a poem where the woman
    is the despised and loving creature
        for a change.

# DIANA AND ACTAEON

You only think you see them
  the dolorous dogs of conscience

You hear only yourself
  to have looked at the naked moon

The moon rises again
  under the quicks of your nails

That is the moon's music
  from the far side of a syringe

They are her officers
  the moon team under Doctor Lucubrare

Soon she will come to see you
  she has her times of the month

And memories. Memories of the sun
  things not looked at directly

You looked and fancied and she knew
  now there is no safety anywhere

She gives flowers to a nurse
  for certain she has seen your grave

From the bottom of the lift-well
  the howls of the baskervilles

# KEEPING IN TOUCH

They write these letters. Now from A
   comes shrewd boasting soon seen through;
B types a page about a play,
   A sifts it for a certain clue.

It can't be so, their needs are odd:
   cautious A thinks the world well lost,
he blames his prick, his Mum, his God—
   B likes the feeling not the cost.

But each inside his armoured need
   serves the politics of the flesh;
thirty years' war attends the deed,
   two loves meet identical press-

ure, marry forever in the post:
   A's bitter about so little bed
and B's machine has lost its ghost—
   love is a letter to the dead.

# JOB'S DISCOUNTS

1

I am making my sandcastles of scar tissue
Those crises of feeling were each a death
My doctor says emotions are bad for the heart
My closed hand is the history of the people
My open hand is the individual fate
Somebody would be glad of my two feet


To the peering woodlouse I am *Il Magnifico*
God could not write the biography of a raindrop
Every pig-raising province has its America
It is possible to measure the silence of the heavens
Mercy would not have opened the revenger's grave
I know now that the watching will never stop



2

Dear Uncle Job
              I'm writing this from out of town
I hear that God
              is trying to get you down;
Nothing personal
              just one of his hang-ups,
A bet of sorts
              with the Son of Morning in his cups—
Don't trust Him
              His impartiality is a pose,
He's going out
              with a Communard in panti-hose,
He's real mean,
              as glum as a garfish and bendy
As Pluto the Pup:
              He's new round here, just another trendy.

Did you hear

        how he loused up the Garden job,

Had to get angels

        to clear the squatters with a tear-gas lob;

He's all style,

        I mean He says they mustn't make it

Under the tree,

        then the woman comes on naked

As a split-pea,

        down goes Riley, slipping in the ferns.

He can't eat corn,

        He tells everyone what He earns,

He's a big hater,

        you gotta say nice things about his vowels—

*My Antiphons,*

        *My Tonus Peregrinus,* he howls—

*I want ten per cent*

        *on Job and I want it now!*

That's His style;

        He's on the clover like a cow—

We love you here, Unk,

        we know what the tykes are on,

The big wheat grows

        just where the sun shone.

# THE WORKERS

The people of the meniscus
see over the edge of the world


Valerie runs her hand along Hugues' bright creases
and takes her finger within an inch
of his sleeping penis in Independence Square,
she loves him over coffee and pigeons
and over the complications of her doubt


It takes a whole Black Country
and at least one new oxidizing process
to maintain the canals in her fallen eyelids


Justice of the sun, she says, on the water—
this was once the capital of the wool trade
when the bankers were the nouveaux riches—
calm of the duck-billed dawn
and the cerise and cerulean pills!


Their planes are honed on the sky
and they are together beside the *Geertgen tot Sint Jans*,
a torturer's and a peasant's descendants


On the broad back of money
are the fine moles of sensibility—
she reads that in a novel
and thinks how like a girl in a novel
she is—
      she knows how to
find a switch and turn the room
to a D Major landscape

          she has a vision
that all the rest are in the mines
where the D Major is dug,
the perruked miners,
workers at the star-hot centre
filling the hoppers with life
and she and her lover at the end
of the beautiful cables, fed and balanced
and warmed, thinning down, rarefied
and soon to have wings—
the libraries and the switches and the slurry
are programmed for this,
her delicacy and radiant quickness,
her crystalline migraine which they like ants
are the distant and decent makers of

# THE WIDOW'S STORY

Eight years old the week of Mayerling,
Given the theme 'make life a work of art',
A statue unveiled to Daddy in the Park—
How best use these gifts knowing nothing
That's first rate moves far from the heart?
The waters of death recede from the Ark.

The Styrian genius winks across a room,
Flowers, a *Liedchen*, Hinkel Dinkel the pup—
Great symphonies bleach like cherry seeds in May:
Madness in the sky, the Empress's womb
Honeyed with defeat—you're making up
Games of Europe the young will have to play.

Count Prosit brings the Emperor's regret,
'That Oberon was boiling with *Affekt*,
But why not try America, the Court
Must take cognizance of the Rupprecht Set.'
Forty staved paper for number six, cherries pecked
By blackbirds, love a trade and not a sport.

Memory sets in bits. Your great dead man
Will keep you warm in comfortable exile
But at his bier you only think of bed
With the painter with the stainless steel hand.
Vienna glows at your widow's catherine wheel,
Sparks from your suttee turn the Danube red.

Peace to the architect with Europe on
His hat, peace to the angel daughter dead;
Study instead the little covert Czech,
Forty years a sallow tenor song
Like doctor's oil in your ears—it's said
He bit you where he reached, your pearl-strung neck!

15

Stars over Europe when the bourgeoisie
Get no work and the rumpish corporal plans
His twilight table talk are just the lights
Appropriate to Venice and your fee
For love, but those black stars your lover scans
Burn millions in their distant appetites.

New World and the Old in Beverley Hills,
Club of those that got out—even the Führer's
Favourites are reborn in delayed upbeats;
America is ignored save for two skills,
Publicity and death—instinct for the surest
Way quotes both Eichendorff and Keats.

Austria returns, the beach set fades
Outexiled by fiacres in the rain—
Die Wiener Herrn are at the Studio,
Death sends his card, the little Mill Maid
Dances for the hunter, music again
Plots with the lovers before they weep and go.

# EUROPE
*An Ode*

Breathe honey looking south, the mined land over;
    Tamed temples take the flash of rain
        Buckets up to their gone gods, their many
        Children born stinging like the horsefly—

No lark, no scrap of cirrus, canna flower
    But runs in the veined skull for sap,
        Saints blanket-thrashed to city samplers,
        Angels starved gold in high blisters!

Hefty the face of the Carthaginian, puce
    The blood-flower in his morning steps;
        Just a rock, towelled by tourists, yet sat
        Down there the bum of God and a gold cat.

Crossroads, too, injustice knows them
    Like its uncle's nose: hard men hived
        His sweet spittle, bright the honey
        Of rational Emperors, patrimony

Of ten pathic brothers; dust lies on
    Whig terraces, night road of oratory, mud
        Mentioned us among its peers—
        Lady Holland, operatic cards, tears!

Sun-high, valley-served, in his dressing gown
    Tussling with tyranny in dead March,
        Remarkable for leaves, the great Glans foresees
        A million Fiats in the palms, water-skis

Ploughing by Procida, directors' gutturals
    On tape: 'selfishness of the poor'
        Blows the market, money complains
        Under Swiss peaks, the S.S. Keynes

Founders in a mere fathom. Worm meat
    They all were but gave out with Gothic,
        Clawed from Cluny, struck the sun
        With big verbs—die for a pun

Was one rule, outlive any pain
    Another. Pretty Polis, lisped the Boy King,
        Back to back, whitebait, layer-cake;
        Promises make Jack's jaw ache.

But this was invective, had two ideas
    America and love, that the starved angel
        Blow right the great gold mouthpiece,
        A yes for everyone and the police.

Nations navigated too; who then humped
    Henry in his tower where the great west
        Started, over the black rim, the dark
        Gods and grief? In a letter, Mungo Park

Wrote the brown coast Augustan—alas
    Other evangelists erupted, the white man
        Found his fetish, truth and order
        For bare breasts and turned-on tape recorder.

Leave us love, they said, love is politics,
    Love is poets and prisons, love's
        A revolution, winter on a mattress
        Coughing up Europe's pound of flesh.

They were on a moving staircase and knew it,
    Knew the latter God as Progress and why not?
        A drained fen tins peas and we eat—
        Bulldozers fan out in the heat.

So they found a place to put the Mob!
    It built aristocratic porches
        But sat around psalming—each
        Fallen Fruit fancied itself a peach.

They god-hauled the railroad and they swam
    The capitalist rapids but ended up
        In Printer's Ink with half a gimmick—
        Back to Europe, men, we're stuck!

There for the fallen Gothic Museums glow,
    Enthusiastic doubt like sun motes
        Turns to dandruff on old shoulders:
        At the start of the world, the beholders

Find the permanent kingdom and this
    Peninsula, its rational Europe
        Where the blood has dried to Classic
        Or Gothic, cinema names in aspic.

But the giant iron is ours, too:
    It flies, it sings, it is carried to God—
        We come from it, the Father, maker and healer,
        And from Oviraptor, the egg-stealer,

Launched in the wake of our stormy mother
    To end up on a tideless shore
        Which this is the dream of, a place
        Of skulls, looking history in the face.

# THERE ARE TOO MANY OF US

I see him there, the dedicated man,
His wife in her dressing gown boiling eggs,
Flinty smuts of indignation
Constellated round his eyes—he handles
A letter like a search warrant
And some must burn and some must pay for this;
His choler is how the gods of chance
Fixed the fringes of the world,
A paradigm of the judging sun,
To be a lemon eye in winter
Through liberal mist but finally
To plate the prophet's face with gold.

And victims sitting in the tireless hall
Before the second paper of the afternoon
Are answering shadows. Who'd start
The heron of the Eighteenth Dynasty
From painted reeds; who'd say Paul
To a persecutor from a quarterly?
The blind man is called in as
Adviser and the tone-deaf President
Buy's Wagner's bed—our only protection
Sacred objects with a patina
Of fear. And that there are too many
Of us will never refer to one.

As the great theologian said
There are no special peoples or
Special solutions, only a tradition
Of mind going uphill and always
Getting steeper. The lucky genius
Refines his burden to one thing
At a time—his passenger friends
Are quacking in the beautiful

Incomprehensible languages: doves
Are at the feet of demon anthropologists,
Amazing earthquakes are on
Video tape, nothing is allowed to die.

I respect my red-haired adversary
Cutting his measured and
Unsatisfactory words. Even syntax
Falls from the bone, who would have guessed
That final seriousness is temporal?
The mystery of our sacrifices, our
Faustian bargains, the golden pledges
Of loves we've spent are only
Pitch-pine on a fire: we world-eaters
Are eaten in our turn and if we shout
At the gods they send us the god of death
Who is immortal and who cannot read.

## A CONSUMER'S REPORT

The name of the product I tested is *Life*,
I have completed the form you sent me
and understand that my answers are confidential.

I had it as a gift,
I didn't feel much while using it,
in fact I think I'd have liked to be more excited.
It seemed gentle on the hands
but left an embarrassing deposit behind.
It was not economical
and I have used much more than I thought
(I suppose I have about half left
but it's difficult to tell)—
although the instructions are fairly large
there are so many of them
I don't know which to follow, especially
as they seem to contradict each other.
I'm not sure such a thing
should be put in the way of children—
It's difficult to think of a purpose
for it. One of my friends says
it's just to keep its maker in a job.
Also the price is much too high.
Things are piling up so fast,
after all, the world got by
for a thousand million years
without this, do we need it now?
(Incidentally, please ask your man
to stop calling me 'the respondent',
I don't like the sound of it.)
There seems to be a lot of different labels,
sizes and colours should be uniform,
the shape is awkward, it's waterproof
but not heat resistant, it doesn't keep

yet it's very difficult to get rid of:
whenever they make it cheaper they seem
to put less in—if you say you don't
want it, then it's delivered anyway.
I'd agree it's a popular product,
it's got into the language; people
even say they're on the side of it.
Personally I think it's overdone,
a small thing people are ready
to behave badly about. I think
we should take it for granted. If its
experts are called philosophers or market
researchers or historians, we shouldn't
care. We are the consumers and the last
law makers. So finally, I'd buy it.
But the question of a 'best buy'
I'd like to leave until I get
the competitive product you said you'd send.

## STROKING THE CHIN*
*Some possibilities*

At the same time
emit a thin bat sound,
sitting in the William Morris chair
looking at the Scandinavian blind,
the easiest way into the mountains
and the land of monkey tails.

\* \* \*

Things don't happen this way,
I write them down this way
and I pull from my chin
two hairs I've allowed to grow—
so much for historicism, I say.

\* \* \*

Remembering her sentimentally,
feel to see if I've shaved,
for she wasn't always good-tempered,
being a good fuck but a spiky human being.

\* \* \*

If I centre my thumb
in the almost non-existent
dimple of my chin and touch
my four reachable moles
with my four free fingers
        that brunette
will leave her publisher
and cross the tiled floor
of the restaurant to invite

* Spelt *Ch'in*, this is a Chinese lute. There are a number of acknowledged
ways of playing it, each descriptive of a mood or state of mind. They are
called Ways of Stroking the *Ch'in*.

me back to Montagu Square
for the afternoon.

* * *

In the Lord High Admiral's style,
the other arm leaning on an astrolabe,
elbow on Mandeville and Marco Polo,
watch them bring aboard three trussed Indians,
some dull gold in a nest
of parrot feathers and a vein
of pox for the sake of history—
the belief in progress is worth it.

* * *

Caught between the smell of celery
and the sun's incandescence
on the polished back of a brush
pinch dry flesh at mean temp-
erature, my agreeable dewlap,
and curl up like a Degas print.

* * *

After the oven exploded
I passed for black
and wrote three articles
for liberal journals
and occasioned
a season of old
Eddie Cantor films—
my statue, chin in hand,
is to be erected
in a small South London park
to illustrate the First
Mode of Opportunity.

* * *

Two severed heads
with trailing beards
look out of a
Nineties photograph—
Chinoiserie!

# SUNDAY

Where George Herbert would
Have seen this day the holiday
That made natural the good
In its six forerunners, I only play
A recording of a Lutheran
Cantata and lie in the thick
Enriched simplicity—man
In heaven and God in aspic.
The debate shifts to the garden. Where
Is Eden, the Marketing Man
Is inviting the press to the square
To launch *Summer Days?* In the Underearth
Of the Betrayed Biped I close
My umbrella eyes and it rains
Protestant tears on a big nose. Pains-
taking love leaves me alone
With the *Keyboard Practice* and the *Great
Service.* We come to a place of stone,
Basalt sun on a granite street,
And the Prelude on the Chafing Blood
Is playing; the Holy Nuisance of
St. James's Park stands in St. Crud-
the-Great in the twenty-four colours of love
Chanting the *Song of David* to birds
And beasts and flowers and I wake up
To Sunday in London, to comfortable words
And the Grail filled with orange cup.

# ON STONEBARROW HILL

The whole population of England could fit
Under this gentle sloping hill, if some piper
Led them home to their ancestral shale.
The surf is all above me where the clouds
Race and lock about the pivoting sun:
I lie across the path of dogs and blackberriers
And silver-headed ladies carrying thermoses;
I am on a very infirm crust and doubt
The orthodoxy of this galleried field
Owing so much to God and to the National Trust—
Perhaps I shall be exalted like the noticeboard
Marked Danger or walk the midway air
As the invisible pink dog-rose does,
My mind still ministering to itself, resolved
To keep its grip on metaphors of death
And guessing shrewdly that those trees would say
They have a knack to last the better perhaps
For the growling of the sea beneath
And the panzer bulldozers circling on the hill.

# LET ME BORE YOU WITH MY SLIDES

It's this new colour process—
the world licks the back of our hands,
four of us on the winter sands
squinting at the soft-backed sea.

Brown for Hester in her aviatrix suit,
little girl in love with an iced lolly,
damson for Juliet and melancholy
sniffed and snapped at by the puppy waves.

And we two stand together on the wall
joined by the membrane of one life,
love's face peers between husband and wife,
a cautious colour like afternoon.

# THE SADNESS OF THE CREATURES

We live in a third floor flat
among gentle predators
and our food comes often
frozen but in its own shape
(for we hate euphemisms
as you would expect) and our cat's
food comes in tins, other than
scraps of the real thing and she
like a clever cat makes milk
of it for her kittens: we shout
of course but it's electric
like those phantom storms
in the tropics and we think of
the neighbours—I'm not writing
this to say how guilty
we are like some well-paid
theologian at an American
College on a lake
or even to congratulate
the greedy kittens who have
found their mittens and are up
to their eyes in pie—I know
lots of ways of upsetting
God's syllogisms, real
seminar-shakers some of them,
but I'm an historical cat
and I run on rails and so
I don't frame those little poems
which take three lines to
get under your feet—
you know the kind of thing—
*The water I boiled the lobster in*
*is cool enough to top*
*up the chrysanthemums.*

No, I'm acquisitive and have
one hundred and seven Bach
Cantatas at the last count,
but these are things of the spirit
and my wife and our children
and I are animals (biologically
speaking) which is how the world
talks to us, moving on the billiard
table of green London, the sun's
red eye and the cat's green eye
focussing for an end. I know
and you know and we all know
that the certain end of each of us
could be the end of all of us,
but if you asked me what
frightened me most, I wouldn't
say the total bang or even
the circling clot in the red drains
but the picture of a lit room
where two people not disposed
to quarrel have met so
oblique a slant of the dark
they can find no words for
their appalled hurt but only
ride the rearing greyness:
there is convalescence from this,
jokes and love and reassurance,
but never enough and never
convincing and when the cats
come brushing for food their soft
aggression is hateful;
the trees rob the earth and the earth
sucks the rain and the children
burgeon in a time of invalids—
it seems a trio sonata
is playing from a bullock's

skull and the God of Man
is born in a tub of entrails;
all man's regret is no more
than Attila with a cold
and no Saviour here or
in Science Fiction will come
without a Massacre of the Innocents
and a Rape of El Dorado.

# AT WHITECHURCH CANONICORUM

This is a land of permutating green
and can afford its pagan ghostly state.
Only from the recurring dead between
the well-dark hedge and talking gate
can mystery come, the church's graveyard,
where now the sun tops the stones and makes
shadows long as a man work as hard
to live as he did, rotting there till he wakes.

That he will wake to trumpets they believed
or tried to who bought him ground to hold.
His dead eye takes in the high coiffure of leaves,
the pebble-dash tower, the numbers in gold
upon the clock face. For once he has reason—
this undistinguished church, whose frown
lies in the lap of Dorset rebuking each season
its appropriate worldliness, has a saint, pale and home-grown.

Saint Candida, white in her Latin and cement tomb,
has lived here since rumour was born.
A woman's pelvis needs only the little room
of a casket to heal the flesh it was torn
from: an enlightened bishop lifted up her lid
and pronounced her genuine, a lady's
bones who if she healed as they say she did
I ask to help me escape the further elbowing of Hades.

I tried to put once, while no one was about,
in the holes for the petitioners' limbs,
the front of my trousers, for love locked out
not impotence, and spoke to that air which held hymns
like amber from the stained glass sides
a prayer to the saint to be given love
by the person I loved. That prayer still resides
there unanswered. I gave the iron-studded door a shove

and stood again among the unsaintly dead.
St. Candida is also St. Wite,
the Latin derived from the Saxon misread,
the death clothes she sings in as bitter
to her as when her saintly heart stopped.
England has only two saints' relics confirmed
and hers are one. Three times now I've dropped
by at Whitechurch and asked her her easiest terms

for assistance. The old iron trees tend to roar
in the wind and the cloud seems unusually low
on the fields, even in summer. The weight of before
stands here for faith; so many are born and go
back, marvellous like painting or stones:
I offer my un-numinous body to the saint's care
and pray on my feet to her merciful bones
for ease of the ulcer of feeling, the starch of despair.

# ON THIS DAY I COMPLETE
# MY FORTIETH YEAR

Although art is autonomous
somebody has to live in the poet's body
and get the stuff out through his head,
        someone has to suffer

especially the boring sociology of it
and the boring history, the class war
and worst of all the matter of good luck,
        that is to say bad luck—

for in the end it is his fault, i.e. your fault
not to be born Lord Byron and saying
there has already been a Lord Byron is no excuse—
        he found it no excuse—

to have a weatherboard house and a white
paling fence and poinsettias and palm nuts
instead of Newstead Abbey and owls and graves
        and not even a club foot;

above all to miss the European gloom
in the endless eleven o'clock heat among
the lightweight suits and warped verandahs,
        an apprenticeship, not a pilgrimage—

the girl down the road vomiting dimity
incisored peanuts, the bristly boss speaking
with a captain's certainty to the clerk,
        'we run a neat ship here':

well, at forty, the grievances lie around
like terminal moraine and they mean
nothing unless you pay a man in Frognal
        to categorize them for you

but there are two sorts of detritus, one a pile
of moon-ore, the workings of the astonished
mole who breathes through your journalism
        'the air of another planet',

his silver castings are cherished in books and papers
and you're grateful for what he can grub up
though you know it's little enough beside
        the sea of tranquillity—

the second sort is a catalogue of bitterness,
just samples of death and fat worlds of pain
that sail like airships through bed-sit posters
        and never burst or deflate;

far more real than a screaming letter,
more embarrassing than an unopened statement
from the bank, more memorable than a small
        dishonesty to a parent—

but to make a resolution will not help,
Greece needs liberating but not by me,
I am likely to find my Sapphics not verses
        but ladies in Queensway,

so I am piling on fuel for the dark,
jamming the pilgrims on tubular chairs
while the N.H.S. doctor checks my canals,
        my ports and my purlieus,

praying that the machine may work a while
longer, since I haven't programmed it
yet, suiting it to a divisive music
        that is the mind's swell

and which in my unchosen way
I marked out so many years ago
in the hot promises as a gift I must follow,
       'howling to my art'

as the master put it while he was still young—
these are the epiphanies of a poor light,
the ghosts of mid-channel, the banging doors
      of the state sirocco.

## THE SANITIZED SONNETS
*A continuing sequence*

I

Somebody must have been telling lies about Porter
for they took away his sense of pitch
and they wouldn't let him scratch his itch
and they put a strain on his aorta

and they said he suffered from Porter's Complaint,
i.e. an inability to feel anything when feeling
is the whole point of the operation—try kneeling,
they said, your old father's a secular saint.

And they told him to report to the tower.
It was all green and phoney along the Yeats-like land,
death was leaving on the hour—

the hand down the front, the trusted kiss was a lie—
he wrote this on his girl's letter in a shaky hand
'I haven't enjoyed life. I don't want to die.'

**2**

It's there, somewhere in the Platonic cold store,
the work of art all computers love,
very Greek, very rational, yet so much more—
a Mahlerian *Abmarsch* perfected from above.

And the perfection floats in professors' hair,
ends up as a well-displayed and priceless junk:
the luckier art is remade in the air,
holy bubbles mark where Schönberg sunk.

A page is turned—eureka, a snatch of tune
is playing itself, the piss-proud syllables
are unveiling a difficult prosody,

two unclean bodies are seeking pleasure—the moon
goes into Alcaics; at six bells
Agamemnon comes into the bathroom to die.

3

Heterodoxy's your doxy and orthodoxy's
my doxy. I scriven at my inlaid desk
in a too-new world. Now memory, cut and mix. The Esk
in Autumn was cold gold with leaves. Biloxi's

been blown down by hurricane, Camille,
two hundred dead. Frightened of tumours
which were itchy spots, blessed by rumours
that Ad. Reinhardt is a poem pack. Veal

I won't eat, but otherwise I'm selfish.
I dream beautiful music with dirty words,
your legendary spoor. 'Beered and belchish

come I to the bosky core; none is near,
yet here entangled by the whiting birds,
on mark and fen find singletons of fear.'

4

Much have I travelled in the realms of gold
for which I thank the Paddington and Westminster
Public Libraries: and I have never said sir
to anyone since I was seventeen years old.

I've wasted forty years thinking about
what to write on my gravestone. Here lies
five foot eleven, thirteen stone, brown eyes,
who got his tenses wrong and his zip caught.

He had a high temperature called mother
and knew the Köchel catalogue by heart,
he is the programmers' A. N. Other

but I in my first person present will
do my duty as a consumer of art—
Milton! Dryden! Shakespeare! Overkill!

## 5

Ululate from high wires and the house eaves, doves!
You are my John Cage, my feet in the sky,
my everyday bit of Zen. *Man you must die
like us Turteltauben and our tufted loves.*

This sonnet picks up words like a comb
does paper; *bei Spiel und Scherz bleibt
froh das Herz* and beer froth has wiped
away tears of *Gesellen* far from home.

*Ut, re, sol, la—In hydraulis*—virtuosity
of the west nowhere near Vilayat Khan
on the sitar—the height to me

of western melisma is the oboe ritornello
of the soprano aria from Cantata 187 by Johann
Sebastian Bach. I would not cook on *my* cello.

## 6

Now it's in all the novels, what's pornography to do?
Stay home where it's always been—in the mind.
It's always been easier to wank than to grind,
yet love is possible, palpable and happens to you.

It's nice to have someone say thank you afterwards
goes the old joke. But are the manual writers
right, are masturbators nail biters?
(Even the Freudians are anti, albeit in long words.)

Don't burn *Office Frolics* and *I've a Whip in my Valise*;
in other disciplines the paradis artificiel
is considered high art and not mental disease

and if your mind arranges tableaux with girls—
e.g. strip poker with big-breasted Annabel—
it's a sign the world's imperfect and needs miracles.

7

Man is social and should live alone/
I disappoint you/ what is hate?/ hate is
this disappointment/ we are here to quiz
the infinite/ underneath is common bone

*There* are the smiling daughters/ a linnet
surprises the starlings/ the hot ball rides
over laughter/ the sun has made two brides/
I haven't cried for years/ I could this minute

Nasty the scrapes we get into/ as Darby & Joan
told the TV Interviewer, we've been together
too long/ death has an earphone

He sees a mistress turn into a judge/
marriages are made in the grave/ bad weather
in the soul for ever/ the door will not budge

8

Via the car radio Christ cries I thirst,
a stupid sheep has slipped in the ditch
and bleats to the indifferent marsh. Which,
asks the spirit of midday quarrels, came first,

God or Pain? Home is where the hawk rises
but I lie down with the panting dog.
I stay near the sun, dependent; in my log
I work on punishments and pardons, the assizes

of everyday. In a dream I told
my inquisitors I was a phrase in A Minor
and My Master's Voice. They said *Untold*

*Variety* and *Matchless Cider*, Hungarian Musicians,
were asking for me. Vanished world! I combine a
death with a life and am the sum of precisions.

9

Backwards went the barefoot sage: he chanted
to the hedge birds and fell over the cliff,
the chronicles showed what could be done with an 'if',
winds still storm the trees he planted.

Faster went the Athenian boat but faster still
went death. There will never be equality
until we are all equally loveable: I
won't allow it and history won't allow it. The last evil

is still in the box. The tourist holds his breath
as the white island with sails starts
from the sea. More death, more peace, more death.

The island is a sheet fold on fold
in the sun, the home of pruning and the arts:
sacred ground, so keep your god under control.

10

Anima of birds, I enter at your face/
you walk greenly belittled, the Venus
of ships and men/ to invent the world with your penis
is god-like/ will it be your place or my place?

I made love to my own body to make love
to yours/ we are two people lost in the sweet
of ourselves/ under the table our knees meet/
the nearness burns/ like a god, keep off!

The blowfly drowns in the measured pot
of jam/ the barley sugar never gets out of
the bottle/ the iron will not stay hot.

A lover took nothing to bed here/
the pain is in the words/ 'I fell into love
like a cockroach into a basin'/ love is fear.

Put me in the abbatoirs where the electric poleaxe
runs/ I'll be steak and glue for your sake,
hide and blood for your blue hands/ take
me to the tax haven of twenty heart attacks.

My tongue strokes you/ I am the machine
that works the holy pen/ I need time to please/
analeatorypulseofpossibilities/
there are four seasons here and yet the scene

is always winter/ waughs and lecturing!/
homeoftranscendentalmiddlemen/
be loving then/ then loving be/ be then loving.

While the heart lasts the search is sex/
U/ 2/ my heart is yours to hold again,
'luxuriously bound in rich red skivertex'.

# ADDENDUM TO QUARLES EMBLEMS

Fallen world! however well you bridge it
The warning gap appears in every digit:
Numbers are cyphers, you net them for a sign—
Decimal death moves points from nought to nine.
In O the final eye regards its prey,
After mere one its minion millions play
And on the right of equals signs declares
Infinity and nothingness are pairs.
1 has the sin of Eden on its face,
Until another came there was no place;
Above the line, below or where it sits
Caters for nothing and calls nothing quits.
The following digit brings rebellion in—
2 is addition, knowledge, love and sin,
The cherished first-born indivisible,
Dual Heaven tantamount to Hell.
New 3 names God and then adultery,
Is always extra to the you and me
Yet wakes the Triad from its sleep of sound:
Air above, earth beneath, sea around.
Turn that concourse from your reason's door,
Death, Judgment, Hell and Heaven 4
Last Things, four riders make a bran of dust,
Four corners for a world, a forlorn lust.
Life and death are one, the senses 5;
In atrophy who'll prove you're still alive?
Eyes' trust, tongue's track, ears' words, skin's love, nose's
Knowledge can't tell carcases from roses.
We've gone half way, the first complacent licks
At reason's sores can start. Twice at 6
The day turns over, the tide of dark or light
In the mind's mirror is night's day, day's night.
Six days shalt thou labour building Heaven,
Valhalla rests on sweat: the number 7

Chills the Gods upon their feasting thrones,
Again the revolution is postponed.
Which brings in turn that cottage-loaf, the 8,
Invertible, it shows that love is hate,
Turned sideways simulates infinity,
Egg-timer of our short mortality.
Now to the ultimate digit, the bright 9
Whom double figures hunger to consign
To democratic harness, till the end enthuses
On the months of growth, the number of the Muses.
From these ten digits every stern statistic
Waves its shade on technocrat and mystic;
Unnumbered and unknown we take the light,
Hunt with living numbers, sink from sight.

# MORE FROM MARTIAL

## I, XLIII

What a host you are, Mancinus;
there we were, all sixty of us,
last night, decently invited guests
and this was the order of dishes
you pampered us with:
>  NO late-gathered grapes
>  NO apples sweet as honeycomb
>  NO ponderous ripe pears lashed to the branch
>  NO pomegranates the colour of blowing roses
>  NO baskets of best Sasnia cheese
>  NO Picenian jars of olives


Only a miserable boar so small
a dwarf could have throttled it
one-handed. And nothing to follow,
no dessert, no sweet, no pudding, nothing . . .

>  We were the spectres, this was the feast,
>  a boar fit for the arena, duly
>  masticated by us—

>  I don't want to see you struggle
>  in your turn for a share of the crackling—
>  no, imitate instead
>  that poor devil Charidemus
>  who was shredded in the ring—
>  rather than miser eats boar
>  lets have boar eats miser:
>  *bon appetit*, my host of nothings,
>  I can almost feel the tushes in your throat.

## I, LXXI

Here's a toast to the ladies—
six tiltings of the jug
To Laevia, seven for Justina,
five for Lycas, four Lyde
and three for Ida: one for
each letter of our mistress' names—
too bad the bitches never come,
so five up-endings of
Falernian more—that'll be enough
to call the girl who never fails,
warm-tailed and celerious sleep!

## II, LII

Dasius, chucker-out
at the Turkish Baths,
is a shrewd assessor;
when he saw big-titted
Spatale coming, he decided
to charge her entry for three
persons. What did she do?
Paid with pride of course.

## II, LIX

Small and select, the restaurant called *The Mouthful*
    Overlooks Caesar's tomb and you may view
The sacred domes with garlic on your breath.
    Wine and dine there if you've got the pull,
See and be seen, for even as you chew,
    The God Augustus welcomes you to death.

## II, LXX

Our fastidious friend Cotilus is not fond
of the public baths. You've no idea,
my dear, who's been in before you,
he says, and lets his face wrinkle up
at the prospect of unnamed pollution.
I don't mind, if I can be sure
I'm the first, he admits, scraping
a toe along the water's skin.
To make your prophylaxis certain, Cotilus,
don't wade in, take a running dive
and get your head under before your prick.

## III, XII

At dinner yesterday the smell was heaven
As we sat down to dine at seven;
Fabullus, our host, splashed the place with perfume,
More like a boudoir than a dining room,
But when it came to time to carve
He just sniffed the air and let us starve.
Fabullus, I said, please mind my seat,
I'm off to buy a winding sheet—
To be anointed but unable to ingest
Is the fate of a corpse, not of a guest.

## III, XXII

Twice thirty million sesterces spent
In the service of his famous stomach
Apicius followed where his money went
Under a wide and grassy hummock.

He'd counted his wealth and found there were
Ten million left. Mere hunger and thirst!
Soon life would be more than he could bear
So he drank a beaker of poison first.

Romans are noble in everything—yes,
Even Apicius, the notorious glutton.
He died for his principles—to eat the best
And deny the very existence of mutton.


## III, XXXV

Instant Fish
by Phidias!
Add water
and they swim.


## IV, XVIII

Near the Vipsanian columns where the aqueduct
    drips down the side of its dark arch,
the stone is a green and pulsing velvet
    and the air is powdered with sweat
from the invisible faucet: there winter
    shaped a dagger of ice, waited till
a boy looked up at the quondam stalactites,
    threw it like a gimlet through his throat
and as in a murder in a paperback the clever
    weapon melted away in its own hole. Where
have blood and water flowed before from one wound?
    The story is trivial and the instance holy—
what portion of power has violent fortune
    ever surrendered, what degraded circumstance

will she refuse? Death is everywhere
    if water, the life-giving element,
will descend to cutting throats.


V, X

As you know, Regulus, men are pharisaical,
They're always whoring after the classical;
They read but never praise our living writers
(Though the classics hit them like St. Vitus).
For them the time's always out of joint
And the past, being past, can't disappoint.
How they claim they miss those shady halls
Of Pompey's; or despite the balls—
Up Catulus made of the restoration
Of Jupiter's temple for a grateful nation,
How the fogies praise it because it was done
Back sometime around the year One;
Remember what Rome read in Virgil's time,
Old Ennius and the primitive sublime;
Go further down in the collective past,
Who thought Homer was going to last
And in that fashionable sump, the theatre,
Who fancied Menander a world beater?
Recall, if you can without apoplexy,
The lifetime of Ovid, so smooth and sexy,
The greatest Roman stylist only read
By Corinna, his mistress, and then in bed.
Such Injustice! but hang on a second,
Is that Fame, that creature that beckoned,
With slatted sides and a charnel breath
And a club badge saying *Kiss Me Death*?
Then wait a while, my books, I'll stay
Alive and unknown another day—
If I can't be famous till I'm dead
I'm in no great hurry to be read.

## VII, XVII

How bucolic a biblioteque
where the charmed reader looks out
over raspberry canes
on the encroaching city! If
in these rural stacks there's room
among the heavyweight authors
for the sort of poem which delights
sophisticated Thalia (say a shelf
between the national epics
and the medical encyclopaedias),
then receive these seven modest
books, with the author's latest
emendations (these alone
will enable your heirs to sell them
to a North African University)—
take them, friendly space of
truth and learning, and guard
them well, for by these inconsequential
gifts the world will come
to honour the country library
of Julius Martialis, man
of taste and friend to genius.

# REAL PEOPLE

### 1

swallowed a bottle
of turps substitute
and did irreparable harm
to a masterpiece
    in his stomach
leaving an inexplicable
fashionable rectangle
    on canvas

### 2

his tenure
raised the Merrieweather
Praiseworthy Bank
to top position in the county
    alas, it did nothing
for the game of a country boy
who had been handicap ten
    at seventeen

### 3

this Swordfish pilot
survived Taranto
and three reshuffles
of the B Directors
    when the nerves
of his colon failed
they put in five inches
    of inert plastic

4

what is symbolic
of his thrusting nature,
his pointed nose
and supporting bone structure
        is rat-like
timorous but assertive
and conducive to asthma
        in his marriageable daughter


5

with Rimbaud and Schönberg
as heroes, he was considered
for ten years after university
the authority on Neglected Genius
Vindicated by Time
        his later personality
is just as authoritative
being a demonstration by career
of the alarming corollary
Sponsored Mediocrity is
        Always Up to Date


6

why a stone garden
in an iron town,
cheap clock, rare rain,
        elastoplast on a knee
and an empty swing
        slowing down?

7

this is a little girl
and she lived in a house
with a cat and a terrapin
and a big sunflower
        called Mummy
and the sun was shining
and there was a queen
who caught crabs with oxygen
but daddy didn't come
because he lived too deep
        even for oxygen


8

the choice was there
Socrates or Jesus
        or Insurance
or to be discovered
Heaven's lightning conductor
with only his feet
sticking out
        of a bed of asters


9

Stella had a journal
written for her
the star of the world
        our Stella
had a journalist
write about her
when she got off the boat
in mid-crossing,
the water
        a field of stars

10

The irascible poet
with weak eyes
accuses these reasonable
faces in the street
of being merely
imitations of the perfect
collection of monsters
in his heart


11

Even the 'way out'
doesn't get a cheer
in this reviewer's
piece, but he's worth it
to the magazine,
the way he tells
how he lays
his girl among
the review copies


12

In the chartreuse
glow of the tropical
fish tank, the doctor
tells me his good news:
the better the new cures
the longer the teeth
of the thing that
gets you in the end

13

Where his grandfather
was speared by natives
the young farmer takes
parties of tourists
water ski-ing


14

Uncle Stefan likes to choose
his trout from the live tank,
Uncle Max is kept alive
by a lung in a tank


15

How can one represent
one's profession,
being neither the smelly
monster from the Sleeper's Den
with his prize pile of bones
nor the beautiful young man
landing miraculously
on one lung?

# JAPANESE JOKES

*for Anthony Thwaite*

In his winged collar
he flew. The nation wanted
peace. Our Perseus!

William Blake, William
Blake, William Blake, William Blake,
say it and feel new!

Love without sex is
still the most efficient form
of hell known to man.

A professional
is one who believes he has
invented breathing.

The Creation had
to find room for the exper-
imental novel.

When daffodils be-
gin to peer: watch out, para-
noia's round the bend.

I get out of bed
and say goodbye to people
I won't meet again.

I sit and worry
about money who very
soon will have to die.

I consider it
my duty to be old hat
so you can hate me.

I am getting fat
and unattractive but so
much nicer to know.

Somewhere at the heart
of the universe sounds the
true mystic note: Me.

# APPLAUSE FOR DEATH

Hello everybody here today,
Death has come to say his say;
I'm sure you'll all join with me
In welcoming him to our comity,
So a big hand please, Rotarians—
He's the blondest of Aryans,
The zingiest, stripiest Wasp in town,
He beats Guinness hands down
For Black Power, his Civil Rights
Are sexy as a pair of stretch tights;
We're lucky to get him, I know he's scary
But there's no-one so contemporary—
He's a documentary on the pox
Complete with interviews on the box,
Or a brave face smiling at the screen
On the other end of a kidney machine,
He's ten sparrowhawks laid in a row
Where the I.C.I. insecticides go,
He's the British Farm, that *tabula rasa*,
As flat and hedgeless as a plaza,
He's a foggy evening on the M4,
That Biafran you found a bit of a bore;
Have you ever received his mailing shot
Both for and against the use of pot,
Or read his 'plague on both your houses'
Or 'who in your marriage wears the trousers?'
He thinks Mr. and Mrs. Oedipus Rex
Classic examples of Unisex,
His hand-held camera rather blurs
The charnel distinction of HIS and HERS
But let him loose in a catacomb
Where the infant dead are still in bloom
And the lawyers hang in debating rows
As grave as a line of Latin prose,

He'll draw you the finest possible lines
Through putrefaction's visible signs.
He keeps his iconography
As orthodox as the B.B.C.
But he'll let religion and priests transfigure
His nature (it makes his triumph bigger)
So there's mileage yet and a clear road
For German composers on their *Tod*—
In English he only rhymes with 'breath'
To poets' annoyance, that is unleth
You lisp your way through the double esses
(His favourite poet's the one who confesses).
He has his happenings: the ICA
Honours him almost every day
For it pleases the healthy and well-fed
To take their symbols from the dead
And tycoons relaxing on the ranch
Have each his imported Totentanz,
Grocery Kings love painted tumours
As bankers devaluation rumours
And many an art-collecting Tory
Keeps as his pet *memento mori*
Autopsy sketches by a Master
Or amputations worked in plaster.
Death's personalized and custom-built
And sanitized and purged of guilt;
He's mid-atlantic as Sargasso,
As everlasting as Picasso;
Death is a cheap-flight, short-hop Jumbo,
The home-brewed whisky of Colombo,
The Reverend Paisley's wild Oates
And Paul VI's more dreadful quotes;
Death dictated *Humanae Vitae*
To the frightened heirs of the first Peter,
Injected a couple of million mice
With toxic blight for Vietnam rice;

He's given a thousand Oxford lectures
And named a score of noble Hectors
Who left the earth like Hemingway
Lighter in animals for their stay;
His policy of defoliation
Gave Concrete Poetry to the nation;
His critical triumphs are recorded
In the ten books Leavis lauded
And he'll be there at the wheelwright's shop
When modernity shuffles to a stop.
Things he resembles are: Dr. Husak,
Nixon, factory farms and Muzak,
The edible novel (in marzipan),
The Common Market, the non-stick pan,
Zukofsky's Catullus, anyone's Lorca,
The next long-distance protest walker,
Reformers who finish every speech
With *delenda est* or else 'from each
according to' et cetera,
Sci-Fi Porn, All Bran, The Car
Of the Future, reviewing dons
The *Spectator* takes for silver swans.
Death is as boring as Music Theatre,
Impedance, baffle, Herz and tweeter,
As natty and nasty as Enoch Powell,
Ambivalent as Roberta Cowell;
Death shares the news with Françoise Hardy's
Sex life, Lady Antonia's parties,
Mr. Wilson's thousand days,
*Plots of the World's Most Famous Plays*,
Book Club Medals of J. B. Priestley,
'Your Bed Manners, are they bold or beastly?'
The Customs let him through Heathrow
With a thousand tons of hash in tow;
We need him for our heart transplants,
Our Bollingen, Ford and Fulbright grants;

His corgis and his Christmas speeches
Are reassuring as Doctor Leach's
Praise of our libertarian land
Or the Black Dyke Mills or Foden's Band.
I know he's going to tell us how
It feels to be Mister Here & Now—
Don't twist your fingers in your lap
But give him a really thunderous clap
And remember just one thing before
I let him have the speaker's floor:
When next you meet him after this
You'd better give your wife a kiss,
Pack a few things for eternity
(Polaroid glasses and Pekoe tea)
And say as I'm saying to you now:
I'm ready to go, please show me how,
Is this the place, I think I'm right?
I've finished. Yes. Thank you. Good Night.